W9-CME-318

Busy Machines

Diggers

Written by Amy Johnson

Illustrated by Kirsten Collier

WINDMILL BOOKS ™

Published in 2021 by Windmill Books,
an Imprint of Rosen Publishing
29 East 21st Street, New York, NY 10010

Copyright © 2021 by Miles Kelly Publishing

All rights reserved. No part of this book may be reproduced in any form without permission in writing from the publisher, except by a reviewer.

Find us on

Cataloging-in-Publication Data

Names: Johnson, Amy. | Collier, Kirsten.
Title: Diggers / Amy Johnson, illustrated by Kirsten Collier.
Description: New York : Windmill Books, 2021. | Series: Busy machines
Identifiers: ISBN 9781499485691 (pbk.) | ISBN 9781499485714 (library bound) | ISBN 9781499485707 (6 pack) | ISBN 9781499485721 (ebook)
Subjects: LCSH: Excavating machinery--Juvenile literature.
Classification: LCC TA735.J66 2021 | DDC 621.8'65--dc23
Manufactured in the United States of America

CPSIA Compliance Information: Batch BS20WM: For Further Information contact Rosen Publishing, New York, New York at 1-800-237-9932

Ready to build!

All day long, machines are hard at work on the building site. There are diggers and dump trucks, loaders, and lifters.

Excavator

2

Crane

Concrete mixer

Dump truck

Bulldozer

3

Diggers at work

Most **excavators** have caterpillar tracks that keep them steady on bumpy ground.

Backhoe

A **backhoe loader** has an arm for digging at the back and a bucket for scooping at the front.

Tractor

4

Loader bucket

Monster miner

This is one of the world's biggest machines! It's called a **bucket-wheel excavator**. It is used in mines to dig out huge amounts of soil and rock.

Conveyor belts carry the rock away.

The bucket wheel is attached to a long arm.

The heavy excavator sits on lots of caterpillar tracks that crawl along.

6

Keep it moving

Meet the tough transporters – machines made for lifting, moving, shifting, and scooping.

Forklift

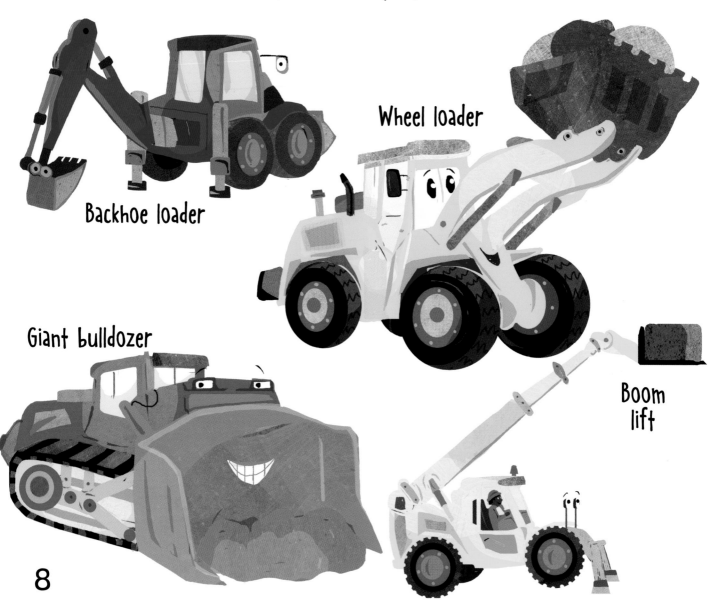

Backhoe loader

Wheel loader

Giant bulldozer

Boom lift

Bulldozer

Dump truck

Skid-steer loader

Log loader

Earth scraper

Tracked loader

9

All about excavators

Munching up the ground, digging holes, and scooping up heavy loads, **excavators** are very busy building machines.

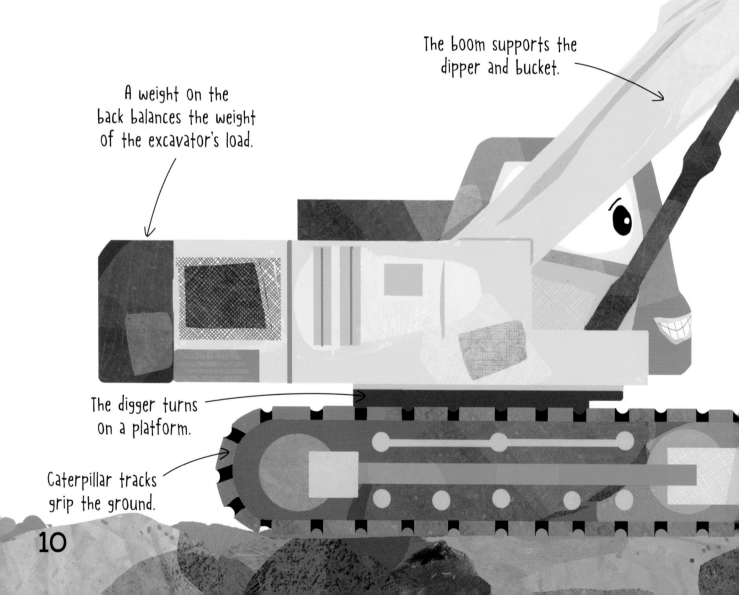

The boom supports the dipper and bucket.

A weight on the back balances the weight of the excavator's load.

The digger turns on a platform.

Caterpillar tracks grip the ground.

The dipper drags the bucket through the ground.

Breaker

Grapple

Drill

The dipper can have other tools attached.

An edge of tough teeth helps the bucket bite into the ground.

Busy machines!

Find your favorite building machine!

13

Rock busters

Deep in a massive pit, it's the job of tough machines to dig rock from the ground.

A rock crusher breaks up big pieces of rock and shoots out smaller bits.

Massive **dump trucks** carry away huge amounts of rock.

Using a big metal blade, **bulldozers** push earth and rock out of the way.

Excavators scoop out rock and load it into the dump trucks.

Wheel loaders move rocks to the dump trucks or the crusher.

Grapples are used to pick up big rocks.

15

sky high

Tower cranes stay in one spot for months at a time, working high above the ground. They help build very tall buildings.

These blocks balance the weight.

The operator has to climb a ladder all the way up to the cab.

This tall tower is called a mast.

The arm is called a jib. It moves up and down and from side to side.

The main arm is called a boom.

All about dump trucks

One of the biggest building machines, **dump trucks** are always on the go. They carry great piles of earth, rubble, and rock.

The box tilts up to let its load slide out.

Huge tires give plenty of grip.

The canopy protects the cab and engine from falling rocks.

Powerful engine

There are ladders for the driver to reach the cab.

19

On the road

A new road is taking shape. Massive earthmovers have cleared the way – now it's time to start building!

1 Dirt is added. **Bulldozers** move and shape the earth.

2 The **grader** uses its long blade to make a flat surface.

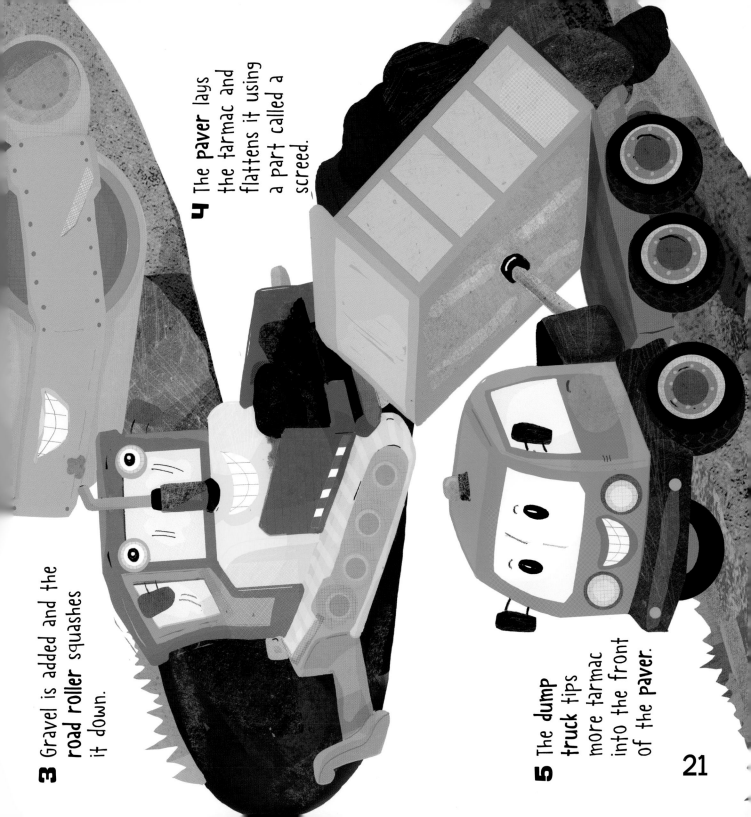

3 Gravel is added and the **road roller** squashes it down.

4 The **paver** lays the tarmac and flattens it using a part called a screed.

5 The **dump truck** tips more tarmac into the front of the paver.

21

smash, crash, crumble

It takes a crew of demolition excavators to tear old buildings down! They have extra long arms for reaching up high.

First, skid-steer loaders take apart the insides of a building.

Then the **excavators** get to work!

Excavators use different tools for different jobs. I'm a pulverizer. I'm great at chomping through concrete and metal!

Walking wonder

To a walking excavator, no terrain is too tough! It tackles water, unsteady ground, and steep slopes.

On the end of the boom is a bucket or another tool for digging.

The boom can also work as an extra leg, stretching across big gaps.

Having four legs means I can dig in places other machines can't reach!